Hal•Leonard®

CELLO PLAY-ALONG

AUDIO ACCESS INCLUDED

ThePianoGuys
Christmas Together

CONTENTS

To access audio visit:
www.halleonard.com/mylibrary

Enter Code
1182-4574-0083-1262

Audio Arrangements by The Piano Guys

ISBN 978-1-5400-1942-4

EXCLUSIVELY DISTRIBUTED BY

7777 W. BLUEMOUND RD. P.O. BOX 13819 MILWAUKEE, WI 53213

Visit Hal Leonard Online at
www.halleonard.com

Visit The Piano Guys at:
thepianoguys.com

O Holy Night/Ave Maria

O HOLY NIGHT
Words by Placide Cappeau
Music by Adolphe Adam
Arranged by Jon Schmidt
and Steven Sharp Nelson

AVE MARIA
By Charles Gounod
and Johann Sebastian Bach
Arranged by Jon Schmidt
and Steven Sharp Nelson

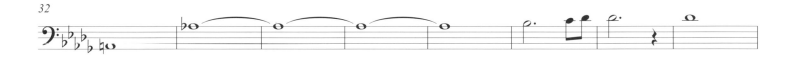

Mary, Did You Know?/
Corelli Christmas Concerto

MARY, DID YOU KNOW?
Words and Music by Mark Lowry
and Buddy Greene
Arranged by Al van der Beek
and Steven Sharp Nelson

CORELLI CHRISTMAS CONCERTO
By Arcangelo Corelli
Arranged by Al van der Beek
and Steven Sharp Nelson

m. 45-46 8va if possible

8va if possible
through m. 65
beat 3   legato

détaché

mp

rall.

rit.

Ode to Joy to the World

As performed by The Piano Guys

ODE TO JOY
By Ludwig van Beethoven
Arranged by Jon Schmidt,
Steven Sharp Nelson and Al van der Beek

JOY TO THE WORLD
By George Frideric Handel
Arranged by Jon Schmidt,
Steven Sharp Nelson and Al van der Beek

8va if possible through m. 78 beat 3

As performed by The Piano Guys

What Child Is This

Traditional
Arranged by Al van der Beek, Jon Schmidt and Steven Sharp Nelson

As performed by The Piano Guys

O Little One Sweet

By Johann Sebastian Bach
Arranged by Al van der Beek,
Jon Schmidt and Steven Sharp Nelson

Moderately slow, expressively

As performed by The Piano Guys

Gloria/Hark! The Herald Angels Sing

GLORIA
Words and Music by Al van der Beek
and Steven Sharp Nelson

HARK! THE HERALD ANGELS SING
Words and Music by
Charles Wesley
Arranged by Al van der Beek
and Steven Sharp Nelson

Moderately slow, in 1

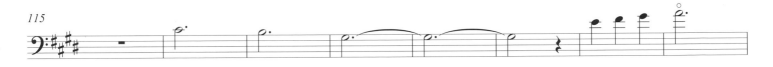

8va if possible through m. 163

8va if possible to end

rit.

As performed by The Piano Guys

The Little Drummer Boy/
Do You Hear What I Hear

THE LITTLE DRUMMER BOY
Words and Music by Harry Simeone,
Henry Onorati and Katherine Davis
Arranged by Al van der Beek
and Steven Sharp Nelson

DO YOU HEAR WHAT I HEAR
Words and Music by Noel Regney
and Gloria Shayne
Arranged by Al van der Beek
and Steven Sharp Nelson

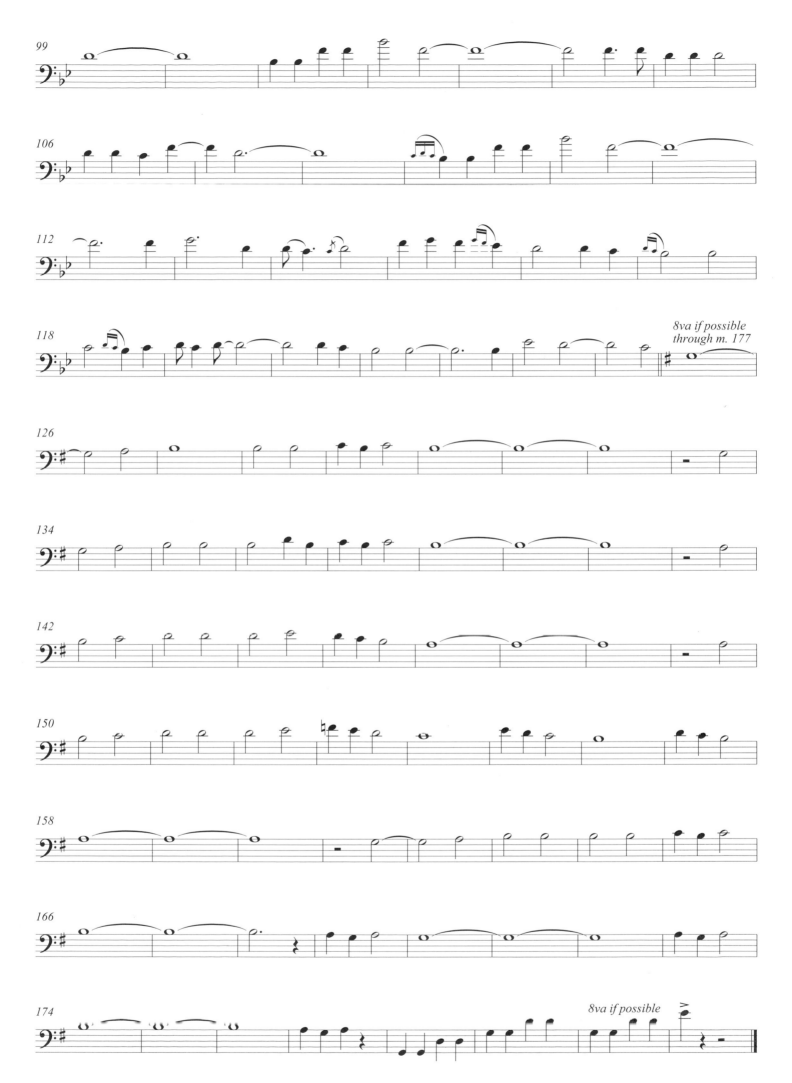

Silent Night, Holy Night

As performed by The Piano Guys

By Franz Gruber
Arranged by Al van der Beek, Jon Schmidt and Steven Sharp Nelson

The Manger

As performed by The Piano Guys

By Al van der Beek, Jon Schmidt and Steven Sharp Nelson

The Sweetest Gift

Words and Music by Craig Aven